The Love of
BIRDS

The Love of BIRDS

John A. Burton
D.H.S. Risdon

octopus

page 1 Little Banded Goshawk *Accipiter badius*
pages 2-3 Mute Swan *Cygnus olor*
pages 4-5 Vulturine Guineafowl *Acryllium vulturinum*
pages 6-7 Orange Chat *Epthianura aurifrous*

First published 1975 by
Octopus Books Limited
59 Grosvenor Street, W1.

ISBN 0 7064 0435 1

© 1975 Octopus Books Limited

Distributed in USA by
Crescent Books
a division of Crown Publishers Inc
419 Park Avenue South
New York, N. Y. 10016

Distributed in Australia by
Rigby Ltd
30 North Terrace, Kent Town
Adelaide, South Australia 5067

Produced by Mandarin Publishers Limited
Toppan Building, Westlands Road
Quarry Bay, Hong Kong

Printed in Hong Kong

Contents

Introduction

Man's fascination with, and love of, birds goes right back through history way back into prehistory. The attitude of peoples living Stone Age lives in the mountains of New Guinea, the Amazon Basin and other parts of the world was probably not that different from the attitude of our own Stone Age ancestors. In all these early cultures birds were, naturally enough, regarded primarily as a source of food, but once sufficient food was available, birds often became pets. The Amerindians will take a parrot from the nest and rear it as a pet; New Guinean Highlanders rear Cassowaries and other birds. These pets serve the twofold purpose of amusing the villagers, particularly the children, and in times of hardship they end up in the pot.

Our own love of birds is not really that much different. Some birds — such as ducks, geese, chickens and gamebirds — are useful as a source of food, while others we delight in for the pleasure we obtain from merely observing them, either as domestic pets, such as canaries or budgerigars, or in the wild. The powers of mimicry of the parrots, the spectacular plumage of the pheasant family, the graceful flight of the swifts and swallows are just a few of the characteristics which man enjoys. The birds illustrated in this volume give some idea of the range of variation to be found, though by no means all the different types can be illustrated.

How is it that birds have managed to colonize almost the entire world? Birds evolved from reptiles but, unlike living reptiles, they are warm-blooded. Their blood temperature is in fact higher than that of most mammals (they live at a faster rate) and in order to keep their temperature at a constant level they have an insulating layer of feathers. 'Featherlight', these keep the bird warm, while adding the minimum amount of weight. Birds' feathers fall into two major groups, the soft down feathers (the warm sweater) and the waterproof and airtight outer coverts (the jackets). This insulation is so efficient that birds are the only warm-blooded animals which are able to breed in the howling wastes of the Antarctic continent during the winter.

Apart from clothing birds, feathers also provide the bird with an extremely efficient method of propulsion: flight. The main feathers of flight are obviously those of the wings, but the tail feathers are almost equally important as an organ of balance. The flight feathers are rather different from those covering the body; they are much stiffer as, in effect, they have to support the weight of the bird. The masters of the air, such as albatrosses, swifts and Frigate Birds, have long narrow wings on which they are able to glide for hours, making only slight movements. The scimitar-winged Needle-tailed Swift can fly at over 100 miles an hour (161 km/h). Other birds, among them the game birds, have short, rounded wings and are consequently not capable of long sustained flight; on the other hand, they can accelerate very rapidly, which is all that is normally necessary to enable them to escape predators.

There are a number of birds which have lost the power of flight, and some which rarely use it. Many of the gamebirds, waterbirds and seabirds only use their powers of flight in an emergency, preferring to run at all other times. The largest birds in the world are all flightless: the Ostriches, the Emus, the Rheas and the Cassowaries have all independently lost the power of flight in the course of their evolution. The title of largest flying bird is difficult to award: the condors and albatrosses both have wingspans which approach 12 feet (3.7

m), but they are lightweight in comparison with the smaller-winged Trumpeter Swan and Great Bustard, which may weigh nearly 40 pounds (18 kg).

As can be imagined, the wear and tear on a bird's feathers is pretty severe. and birds keep their plumage in trim by moulting their feathers at regular intervals, usually once or twice a year. Some birds, such as waterfowl, may actually become flightless for a period while the flight feathers are renewed.

Feathers are not only necessary for flight and insulation: they are also colourful and the colour has a function. In some species, for example, the nightjars and the females of many gamebirds and ducks, colour is used for camouflage. In a great many species there is a considerable difference between the plumage of the two sexes (sexual dimorphism), the female almost invariably being the dowdier to help conceal her while incubating the eggs. The male has often developed elaborate plumes for display, several forms of which are illustrated in this volume.

The form of birds often reflects their habits: long-legged birds are almost invariably ground-dwellers, and in many cases they live in water habitats. This applies whether the bird is a small wader, such as a stilt, or a gangling flamingo. In some cases, quite unrelated birds look superficially similar and usually they are found to have similar habitats. The Secretary Bird is quite obviously a bird of prey, with its

hooked beak, yet from a distance, as it strides across the plains, its long legs make it look more like a crane. The vast majority of the world's birds are small. They belong to the group loosely referred to as perching birds or song birds, which includes the sparrows, finches, tanagers, warblers, crows and many others.

Apart from feathers, eggs are another feature that all birds have in common, and it is this that ties all the various species to land at some stage in their lives. Unlike the mammals (such as whales and dolphins) and the reptiles (seasnakes), no bird has complete mastery over the oceanic environment; even seabirds like the albatross have to return to land in order to breed.

While the embryo is developing inside the egg, it is very vulnerable, and to protect the egg, both from predators and the elements, many birds build a nest. Some birds make no nest, laying their egg direct onto bare ground or a rocky ledge, or even the branch of a tree, others make a mere scrape in the ground, while others go to considerable lengths in building the nest. These include the intricately woven nests of the weaverbirds, the wrens and many other small birds, the floating nests of the grebes, the walled prisons of the hornbills, and, the most protected of all, nests made underground or in holes in trees. Although many completely unrelated birds nest in holes (natural holes, or holes excavated by the birds in trees, banks or the ground), they all have one particular characteristic in common: the tendency for the eggs to be white or very pale so that they show up in the dark, preventing accidental breakages.

Throughout the world, birds are disappearing; even if total numbers have not declined, the variety of species is getting fewer and fewer. This is due to a combination of reasons, but the most important single factor must be the expansion of the human population and its consequent effect on the environment. Even a slight increase in the number of humans can be disastrous. Disturbance from hunting and trapping is insignificant in comparison with the effect of clearing forests, polluting water, ploughing up land and pouring on pesticides and other chemicals. Some of the more adaptable birds may actually benefit from the changes wrought by man, but a great many just cannot cope and move slowly, but inevitably, towards extinction.

Fortunately for birds, however, man likes them. He is also usually aware of their decline and more and more effort is being devoted to saving endangered species. Many countries now have societies for the protection of birds and the International Council for Bird Preservation coordinates the activities of conservationists throughout the world. After reading this book and studying the photographs, perhaps you will feel that you too want to help protect the rare species, to ensure that our descendants can still enjoy the variety of birds illustrated in this book.

The world
of birds

The Robin, or Redbreast, *Erithacus rubecula* (bottom right) is Britain's national bird. It was first mentioned as long ago as A.D. 530, when St Mungo performed a miracle by restoring his tame Robin to life after it had been killed by his pupils. In Britain it is a common bird and is often very tame, searching for worms and other small animals within inches of a gardener. Its continental cousins are rarely as tame. Wherever the English have settled, they have taken their affection for the Robin with them and this has resulted in unrelated birds showing a vague resemblance to the English Robin being given the same name. There are 'robins' in India, North America and Australia.

The so-called Robin of North America *Turdus migratorius* (top right) is in fact a large migratory thrush. As can be seen from the photograph, it really bears only the very slightest resemblance to the real Robin. It is, however, like the European bird in that it is an adaptable species; although originally a bird of the forests, it has not only managed to survive the extensive felling of the woods and forests, but has moved into areas where it was previously unknown. Like its British counterpart, it is often tame and trusting towards man and has moved into many parks and gardens.

The early settlers in Australia noticed pretty little robin-sized birds, some of which had brilliant scarlet breasts, and to these they gave the name 'Robin'. When the first naturalists began studying the birds of Australia they found that these red-breasted 'Robins' were related very closely to a number of equally brightly coloured birds — some black and white, some rich orange, some bright yellow and some bright pink. The whole group of birds kept the name 'Robin'; hence the Pale Yellow Robin *Eopsaltria capito* shown in the illustration (left) which lacks any colour remotely resembling red!

Among the world's most fascinating birds are Africa's huge family of weavers, which also includes the familiar sparrows. Some of their nests are elaborately woven and beautiful. The architect is usually the male weaver-bird, whose courtship often begins after he has built the nest.

A day or two may elapse before the nest, tightly woven out of vegetable fibres, is completed, and when it is ready it will be securely anchored to its twig or branch. The entrance may be a hole near the bottom or by means of a narrow tube. To attract a mate, some weavers hang upside down from the bottom of the nest and execute a series of eye-catching acrobatic turns to the accompaniment of unmusical chirps. Others may cling to the side, chattering and chirping loudly. Although most weavers are quite noisy birds, few have any real song.

If the hen is interested, she will show her approval of the nest in a practical fashion by flying straight inside and taking up residence. Some kinds of weaver, the Village Weaver *Ploceus cuccullatus* (right), for instance, are in such a hurry to start a new nest for a second partner that they only wait long enough for the hen to settle on her eggs before moving off.

Village Weavers are gregarious birds, nesting in large colonies. They select a tree, sometimes quite close to a village, and load the branches with their beautiful suspended nests until the tree looks as if it is growing strange, exotic fruits. Throughout the year, the colony remains faithful to its original building site, and there is much coming and going as the birds forage for the seeds and insects on which they chiefly live.

Unique among weavers is the Social Weaver *Phileiairus socius*. These birds live up to their name by banding together, sometimes in their hundreds, to build their amazing communal nests (above right).

As soon as a suitable tree has been chosen, the birds set to work. Their united efforts produce a huge thatched roof of grasses and reeds in the branches, under which the weavers have their own individual nests.

After so much effort, the nest is only used once. By the time the next mating season has arrived, the birds have all moved house. The waterproof roof still stands and so does the rest of the 'building'; the weavers have simply built on a new extension. In time their communal dwelling takes on the appearance of a native hut as, year after year, it increases in size.

Sometimes, however, disaster strikes. The weight of the extensions brings down the tree and the weavers must move on to another, hopefully even stronger, tree.

Our third picture shows yet another kind of weaver, the Golden Weaver *Ploceus bojeri* (above left), a familiar sight in the villages of East Africa.

Not all birds bother to rear their own young and quite a few species deposit their eggs in the nests of another bird, often quite unrelated. The most famous of all these parasites is the cuckoo but, in fact, not all cuckoos behave in the irresponsible manner of the European species; the Northern American species normally rear their own young.

The Dunnock, or Hedge Sparrow, *Prunnella modularis* (right), is a common foster parent for the European Cuckoo *Cuculus canorus* (inset right), which will even lay pale blue eggs to match those of the Dunnock. The Cuckoo lays her egg in the nest of a Dunnock, warbler, wagtail or some similar-sized bird (she is over 1 foot (300 mm) long) and removes one of the rightful eggs. Only rarely do the nest-owners notice the change, and incubation proceeds as if nothing had happened. The young Cuckoo normally hatches before the other eggs, and immediately sets about throwing out of the nest any other eggs or youngsters. This is a simple reflex action which is stimulated when any object makes contact with certain parts of the Cuckoo. The young Cuckoo can now receive the undivided attention of its foster parents, and within a very short time will have grown larger than them; it is not uncommon to see the foster parent standing on the Cuckoo's head in order to cram food down its ever-open gullet.

The Cowbird *Molothrus bonariensis* of North America (below) is a pure parasite. During the breeding season it is very promiscuous, mating quite randomly and not forming lasting pairs. The female lays her egg in the nest of a smaller bird and, as with the Cuckoo, the Cowbird's egg hatches before the others in the nest, the nestling grows faster and soon starves its nest-mates out even if it does not actually crowd them out. During the summer months, the Cowbird is usually to be seen following, or even riding on, sheep and cattle to catch the insects disturbed by their feet.

Many of the whydah group are also nest parasites, laying their eggs in the nests of the small waxbills. Not only do their eggs resemble those of the waxbill, their young have the same markings in their mouths as young waxbills as it is by these markings that the parent birds identify where to put the food and without them the nestling whydahs might starve. Only the male Long-tailed Widow Bird, or Whydah, *Diatropura progne* (left) has the long black tail from which it gets its name.

The Fantails are a group of nearly forty species of closely related birds found only in south-eastern Asia, the south-western Pacific and some Australasian regions. They are related to the Old World flycatchers and are easily recognized by their habit of cocking their tails. The Rufous Fantail *Rhipidura rufifrous* (top left) is shown here on its nest, fanning its tail. It is found in Australia, the Solomons, New Guinea and a few other islands, in a variety of habitats, including jungle, scrub and mangrove swamps.

The European Wren *Troglodytes troglodytes* (bottom left), the only species occurring in Europe, is known in North America as the Winter Wren to avoid confusion with the other nine species found there. It is thought that the wrens evolved in North America and only colonized the Old World from the New, via the Bering Straits, either during or just after the Ice Ages. In many parts of Europe, the Wren is called the 'king' of birds (this may have originated from confusion with the Goldcrest) and there are many superstitions and rituals connected with Wrens. On Christmas Day in Britain, the Wren was once hunted and then stoned or clubbed to death. This ritual has obvious connections with the Christian ritual of death and rebirth, centred on Christmas and the New Year.

The cock Wren, in spite of its small size, is one of the loudest songsters in the dawn chorus, and is often heard breaking into a short snatch of its trilling song even in the middle of winter. At the onset of the breeding season, the male Wren builds several nests and the female then selects one in which to lay her eggs. The nests are domed and of fairly flexible construction; as the youngsters, which may number up to about fifteen, grow in size, the nest will stretch slightly to accommodate them.

The Reed Warbler *Acrocephalus scirpaceus*, shown here feeding its young (right) belongs to a group of birds which even experienced birdwatchers have difficulty in identifying by sight, and the various Reed Warblers and their relatives are best identified by their song. This is probably also the main way in which the various species identify their mates. Reed Warblers are only found in the Old World where they live in a wide variety of marshy habitats.

Bird-lovers delight in the brilliant colours of the small finch-like tanagers of the New World. There are over 200 species and they nearly all retain their dazzling colours the whole year round. In the tropical jungles of South America the most vivid of these compact, active birds vie in colouring with the gaudy parrots as they fly through the trees.

The diversity in colour of the tanager family is amazing. Many species, such as the lovely Emerald-spotted Tanager *Tangara punctata* (top left) and the Black and Green Tanager *Tangara nigrovirdis* (bottom left), build open cup nests in bushes and trees, but there are also some species which build covered nests. Typical tanagers have short, stout beaks. One specialized group of nectar-eating tanagers, however, have long slender beaks which they use to hold and pierce flowers. Some tanagers are quite competent songsters while others, the blue tanagers among them, can scarcely sing a note.

The blue tanagers are busy little birds with a huge appetite for fruit and berries. They also eat insects which they catch, with amusing dexterity, on the wing. Their nests are shallow cups in trees or bushes and after mating a pair of blue tanagers nearly always stays together for the rest of the year. Frequent visitors to parks and private gardens, they are probably among the best known of all the tanagers. The picture (top right) is of the pretty Blue-headed Tanager, *Tangara cyanicollis*.

Other well-known birds of the New World are the seed-eating cardinals. Perhaps the most popular of all the cardinals is the Red Cardinal *Pyrrhuloxia cardinalis* (bottom right) which is very common in the United States, where it is affectionately known as the 'red bird'. A handsome bird, with its bold scarlet colouring, distinctive crest and stout conical-shaped beak, it is a familiar sight on the outskirts of cities such as New York. The female is easily distinguished from the male, as she is more brown than red.

Most cardinals build shallow cup nests which are similar to those of many of the tanagers, except that they are usually found on or very close to the ground.

The three birds illustrated here are among the most colourful of the species breeding in North America. They are quite unrelated and have very different habits.

The Yellow Warbler *Dendrica petechia* (left) is a summer visitor, arriving in North America when the apple trees are coming into blossom. The male is a loud and persistent songster, singing for most of the day and leaving the female to get on with building the nest. The Yellow Warbler is often parasitized by cowbirds but, unlike many other birds, it does not always accept the intruding egg. Yellow Warblers will often build another nest over the top of the original if it contains the egg of a cowbird; as many as six nests, one on top of the other, each with a cowbird's egg, have been recorded. Once the young have hatched, they grow rapidly, leaving the nest about a fortnight later. Shortly afterwards the Yellow Warblers will set off on their journey south.

The Blue Jay *Cyanocitta cristata* (above left) is common over most of eastern North America, except for the far north, and inhabits both deciduous and coniferous forests. The photograph shows the parent bird removing a faecal sac from the nest. This is the way in which most small birds keep their nests clean and tidy; the young produce their droppings in a sort of natural polythene bag, which is then removed by one of the adults and either eaten or deposited at some distance from the nest. This is important, not so much for reasons of hygiene as for protecting the nest from predators. White droppings in the vicinity of the nest would draw attention to the site.

The Blue Jay is often migratory, particularly in the more northern parts of its range; it is also 'irruptive'. A number of bird species, particularly those occurring in or near the Arctic, undergo irruptions, which are sudden migrations caused by insufficient food for the bird populations. Sometimes these irruptions will take the birds hundreds of miles outside their normal range, and new areas may be colonized.

The third species illustrated is the Cedar Waxwing *Bombycilla cedorum* (above), which is also rather dependent on food supplies for its seasonal migrations, although it is rarely as irruptive as its close relative the Bohemian Waxwing, which is also found in Europe. It takes its name from the coloured wax-like wing tips.

The nestlings are fed almost exclusively on insects, but after they have left the nest their diet gradually changes to fruits, particularly berries. The berries are almost exclusively those of wild plants, so the Cedar Waxwing is rarely harmful to agriculture; in fact, it is often useful to farmers, for during the breeding season it consumes large numbers of insect pests, including the Colorado Beetle and Gypsy Moth.

The small finches and buntings
occur in most parts of the world. They
are often attractively plumaged and
many of them have pleasant songs,
and consequently they are very popular
as caged birds. Many of them can
subsist largely on seeds which also
makes them suitable as aviary birds.

Although buntings are fairly widespread in the northern hemisphere, the
Golden-breasted Bunting *Emberiza
flaviventris* (top left) is one of the
relatively few species which occur in
southern Africa. Its striking plumage
distinguishes it from the other species,
which are often rather dull brownish
birds. It is found in rather dry,
wooded areas.

The Goldfinch *Carduelis carduelis*
(bottom left) is both common and
widespread throughout Europe. It has
also been introduced into many other
parts of the world, including North
America, Australia and New Zealand.
In its native Europe, it can often be
seen on thistles growing on open
ground, particularly on the edge of
farmland. It breeds in hedgerows,
orchards and parklands, and builds
a neat, cup-shaped nest, which is often
very well concealed. The nest is
constructed from fine roots, grasses,
mosses and leaves, and it is lined with
thistledown, feathers and wool.

The nestlings are fed mainly on
insects and their larvae, but once out of
the nest they soon begin feeding on
seeds. The Goldfinch is generally
considered very useful to agriculture
as the seeds on which it feeds are
mainly those which are a nuisance to
the farmer — ragworts, thistles and
other weeds. By late autumn the
Goldfinches and their families have
gathered into flocks, or 'charms' as
they are appropriately known.

The Redpoll *Acanthis flammea*
(top right) is a widespread species
occurring right round the northern
hemisphere, both in the New World
and the Old World. It is a bird of the
temperate woodlands, breeding in the
northern woods; in the Arctic areas it
is usually replaced by a very closely
related species, the Arctic Redpoll.
The planting of conifers in forestry
plantations has led to an increase in
the numbers of Redpolls in many parts
of their range. In winter they are also
often seen on farmlands, but more

commonly they gather in mixed flocks with various species of tits (chickadees) and Siskins. These mixed flocks, which are often noisy with the constant twittering of the various species, are always on the move. They prefer wooded habitats, including birch-woods, orchards, young conifers, and, particularly, alder willow carr. The illustration shows a Redpoll drinking, clearly showing the splash of bright pink-red on the forehead, from which the bird takes its name.

The Gouldian Finch *Chloebia gouldiae* was named after the famous English naturalist and artist who described so much of Australia's wildlife as it was being discovered at the beginning of the last century. It is one of the most colourful of all the finches and occurs in three colour forms: the red-headed (right), the black-headed and, very rarely, a yellow-headed variety. It is a bird of the open dry country of the tropical northern parts of Australia.

Ground birds

Large birds that have lost the power to fly frequently have to rely on their speed to escape predators. One of the fastest running birds, and certainly the largest living bird, is the Ostrich *Struthio camelus,* which stands 7-8 feet (2.1-2.4 m) tall.

Our picture (left) shows a pair of Ostriches. The cock has the handsome black and white plumage, prized by African tribesmen.

Birds of Africa's arid plains, Ostriches travel in small parties, sometimes in the company of antelopes and zebras whose movements disturb the small rodents, snakes and insects which make up a large part of their diet. The Ostrich, however, is notorious for its indiscriminate eating, and some extraordinary items have been found in its gut. Nails, coins, bottle tops and rope have all, at times, been discovered.

The cock usually has three or four hens, which lay their eggs, the largest of any living bird, in a shallow scrape in the sand. Ostriches have a communal nesting arrangement, several hens laying their eggs in the same nest. The eggs are normally incubated by the cock.

Ostriches are wary, suspicious birds, ready to run at the slightest hint of danger. If cornered, they will defend themselves by lashing out with their powerful clawed feet.

Unlike the wary Ostrich, the flightless Emu *Dromaius novaehollandiae* (below) is an inquisitive bird with an appetite for the local farmers' crops which has made it extremely unpopular. Found only in Australia, Emus used to be hunted extensively for their meat, and their large untidy nests of grass and twigs were systematically raided when it was found that Emu eggs made delicious omelettes.

Emus are also fast-running birds, with drab brownish-grey feathers which look like coarse hair. The chicks, however, are attractively striped in black and yellow, an effective camouflage as they move through the foliage on sunlit days.

Bustards make good eating and in parts of the world they have been hunted almost to extinction. In some countries, however, they are now protected by law. Although Africa is the bustards' stronghold, there are a few species in Europe and Asia, among them the resplendent Great Bustard, famous for its spectacular courtship display. There is also an Australian species which is known locally as the 'wild turkey', despite the fact that bustards and turkeys are not related.

Like all bustards, Africa's handsome Kori Bustard *Ardeotis kori* (above) nests on the ground. Bustards are powerful fliers and when they take to the air they fly like cranes with their necks stretched out and their legs trailing behind. However, they are more often seen on the ground, roaming about the grassy plains in small family parties.

Bustards prefer a vegetarian diet, but they will sometimes eat small mammals and throughout their lives consume vast quantities of insects, especially locusts. Their addiction to locusts puts them strongly on the side of the farmers.

Well adapted to its life on the South African veldt, the Kori is a quiet, rather sedate bird, except in the mating season when the cock indulges in fierce sparring battles as he fights off contenders for the hen of his choice. His display is very impressive as he inflates his breast and neck feathers and spreads out his wings until he looks almost twice his normal size. The hen makes little or no pretence at providing a nest but lays her eggs almost always straight onto the ground.

Bustards seem to have very little fear of man which makes them 'fair' game in countries where they are not protected, but, if anything does alarm them, they will

almost invariably choose to run rather than take to the air to escape danger. According to palaeontologists, fossil remains of bustards have been found which date back some 50 million years to the Eocene epoch.

Another swift-running bird is the Cassowary of Australasia and New Guinea which, like the Ostrich and the Emu, has lost its power to fly. The Cassowary, with its distinctive booming call, is a wary bird, more often heard than seen as it moves about the dense undergrowth. The extraordinary bony helmet or casque on top of its feather-less head is thought to serve as a kind of shield against thorns as it runs, head thrust forward, through the bushes. It probably also has some sexual significance. The adults have very coarse, hair-like feathers which may also be of some protection in the tangled underbrush of their jungle home.

Cassowaries are notoriously bad-tempered and aggressive, and if cornered will turn and face their adversary. Their feathers are used in tribal headdresses and on more than one occasion native hunters have lost their lives, killed by slashing blows from the Cassowary's feet, which are armed with long, dangerously sharp claws.

The Australian Cassowary *Casuarius casuarius* (above) is the largest member of the family. Unlike most other large flightless birds, it is mainly found in well-vegetated habitats, including the tropical forests of Australia and New Guinea. It is a good swimmer and will take to water when closely pursued. The hen lays her eggs on a platform nest made of leaves and the chicks have a natural protection in their gay, striped colouring, which blends in with their surroundings.

About the size of a Common Pheasant, the Superb Lyrebird *Menura novaehollandiae* (above) is one of Australia's most famous birds. Only the cock has the fantastic, beautiful tail, which he spreads out and swings over his head during his elaborate courtship dance.

Lyrebirds spend most of their time on the ground but as night falls they fly into the forest trees to roost. They are probably the finest of all the bird mimics, able to reproduce with uncanny accuracy not only the calls of other birds and some mammals, but mechanical sounds as well.

The two birds shown on the right are ground-nesters, as is the lyrebird and both are native to Africa. The Vulturine Guineafowl *Acryllium vulturinum* (top right), so called because its head and neck are featherless and make it look like a vulture, is one of the most colourful of the guineafowls. They are birds of the grasslands and are often seen in the company of zebras and antelopes as they forage for insects.

Another interesting ground bird is the large Ground Hornbill, *Bucoruus leadbeateri* (bottom right), found in Africa. Its grotesque bill is not nearly as heavy as it looks. The Ground Hornbill often nests in small caves in rockfaces or tree hollows but, unlike other members of the hornbill family, does not imprison the hen during the incubation period. Ground Hornbills are birds of the open savannas, moving around in small groups. Apart from colossal quantities of insects, they also eat rats and snakes and will often band together to attack quite a large snake.

These hornbills occasionally come to a somewhat ignominious end. They are caught and killed by native hunters who stuff their heads and use them as a disguise for stalking game.

Long~ legged birds

Every year, as winter approaches, the graceful, long-legged White Stork *Ciconia ciconia* (left) of Europe makes its migratory journey to Africa. When it returns, Europeans welcome it as a joyful harbinger of spring. For centuries these beautiful birds have been looked upon as symbols of marital happiness and good fortune, but today there are only a few villages in northern Europe which still have storks nesting on the rooftops and chimney stacks of their houses; further south they are more common. The villagers often do what they can to encourage these visitations by setting out baskets and wheels for the birds to nest on. The fact that storks pair for life and make excellent parents has no doubt lent credence to the legends which have grown up around them.

With the first hint of spring, the male stork returns to the nest which he vacated the previous autumn. As soon as his partner joins him, the nest-building begins. The male brings the building materials, mainly twigs, earth and grass, which the female carefully arranges into a large platform. Over the years these nests may grow to mammoth proportions, for the new home is nearly always built on the ruins of the old. After the chicks are born, both parents feed them and, when they are about two months' old, the fledglings leave the nest.

Although the famous White Stork is most often depicted on its rooftop nest, much of its time is spent on the marshlands searching for crabs, frogs and fishes which it devours in huge quantities.

Most members of the stork family, which is widely distributed throughout the warmer regions of the world, are attractive birds. This cannot be said of the unprepossessing Marabou, or Adjutant, Stork *Leptoptilus crumeniferus* (right). This large bird of tropical Africa and India feeds mostly on carrion and for this reason its presence is tolerated. It is quite useful to have an unpaid refuse collector on the outskirts of your village! In fact, the Marabou has few enemies for its massive bill is no mean weapon and even the hungry vultures keep a respectful distance. The military title of 'Adjutant' derives from the pompous way these storks strut about.

Famous for their spectacular dancing in the mating season, the elegant, long-legged cranes are found in many parts of the world.

One of the most beautiful of all the cranes is the Crowned Crane *Balearica pavonina* (bottom left) of Africa with its magnificent golden crest of bristle-like feathers. With wings half-spread, it has been photographed in a typical dance pose. Both sexes take part in these elaborate courtship dances and, as the birds hop, skip and jump, they punctuate their movements with gracious little bows to each other. As a piece of additional showmanship, one of the dancing cranes will occasionally toss a stick into the air, catching it in its long slender bill as it falls.

Crowned Cranes feed mostly on insects, and as they move over the soft marshy ground they deliberately stamp their feet to disturb their prey.

Numerous legends and superstitious beliefs surround cranes, based on the fact that it is a long-lived bird. In Japanese mythology cranes are said to live a thousand years or more and so have become symbols of longevity and happiness. The Japanese name for crane is *'turu'* and quite often a baby boy will be named Turuo and a girl Turuko. Japanese brides often wear ceremonial kimonos which are beautifully decorated with cranes.

Cranes normally build bulky nests on or close to the ground and the chicks can run about as soon as they are hatched, although it will be several weeks before they are able to fly. Most species of crane make long migratory journeys to warmer lands with the approach of winter. They take to the air in flocks, flying in 'V' formation, with necks extended and long legs stretched out behind.

Also illustrated are a pair of stately Saurus Cranes *Cyrus antigone* (top left), indigenous to India, and the widespread dainty Demoiselle Crane *Anthropoides virgo* (bottom right). This is the smallest member of the family and is often found in zoos.

Our final picture is of a colony of beautiful Painted Storks *Ibis leucocephalus* (top right). In fact, storks and cranes are not related, though they often look alike as they walk sedately around on their long thin legs.

Birds of the marshlands and lagoons, spoonbills take their name from their extraordinary bills, shaped rather like spoons. These birds are fascinating to watch on fishing expeditions as they wade through shallow water swinging their heads from side to side. They keep their half-open bills partly immersed to collect tiny fishes and insects with the minimum of effort. The African Spoonbill *Platalea alba* (above) is typical of the four species of white spoonbills, which nest on the ground in huge colonies.

The noisy Cattle Egret *Bubulcus ibis* (left) belongs to the heron family and also nests near water. It is indigenous to Africa but it is also found in Europe and America, where it is a very recent colonist. As their name suggests, Cattle Egrets are famous for their association with cattle and other large herbivores. They often ride on the back of cattle and other large mammals, catching the insects which settle on their thick hides, or pouncing on small animals disturbed by their hosts. In return the Cattle Egret keeps a wary eye open for danger, sounding its noisy alarm call in warning.

One of the world's most picturesque birds is the Greater Flamingo *Phoenicopterus ruber* (right), which breeds in scattered colonies in Europe, West India, Asia and Africa. The flamingo's nest is fashioned out of soft mud, which soon hardens. The hen lays her egg in the shallow depression at the top of the tower-like structure and the fluffy chick can hop down and run about a few days after it is born. Greater Flamingos put their young into a communal crêche which can be watched over by only a few adults.

Herons are found in practically all parts of the world, although the greatest variety occur in warmer areas. They are long-legged, long-billed birds, superbly adapted for their mode of life, feeding in water on fish and a wide variety of other aquatic animals, including frogs, crustaceans, small waterbirds and their young. Some species have adapted to other methods of feeding and even other habitats, but water remains the heron's basic habitat.

The Louisiana Heron *Hydranassa tricolor* (left) is common in the coastal saltmarshes of most of North America. It tends to be an 'active' feeder, wading through the shallows on the lookout for frogs, fish and other prey. In contrast, the Grey Heron *Ardea cinerea* (top right) of the Old World, is often a very 'passive' feeder, standing motionless for hours on end waiting for some unsuspecting creature to pass within striking distance of its bill. The third species illustrated, the Green Heron *Butorides viriscens* (bottom right) comes from North America and is also a passive feeder. This heron, however, will also venture into marshland to hunt grasshoppers and other insects.

Because of their diet, herons have evolved several useful features to help them deal with slippery fish and frogs. Apart from modifications to the dagger-like bill, one of the most important features of herons is the way in which they are able to keep their plumage clean, even though they are dealing with slime-covered fish and frogs. The claws of herons are modified along the edge to form a sort of grooming 'comb' with which they clean their plumage. The down feathers beneath the main body feathers break down into powder-down — a sort of talc-like powder which the heron uses in grooming after it has disposed of its messy prey.

The rapid thrust which herons make as they capture their prey is made possible by exceptionally strong muscles attached to an enlarged vertebra in the centre of the bird's neck. These muscles contract, hurling the front part of the neck forward with tremendous force and speed.

Waterbirds

Widely distributed throughout the tropical and warm regions of the world, pelicans are birds of ancient lineage. Large heavy birds, they are not very adept at getting themselves airborne but once this is achieved, they are powerful fliers.

The White Pelican *Pelecanus onocrotalus* (left) is found in south-east Europe, Africa and Asia and is typical of most of the species. Thousands of Brown Pelicans *Pelecanus occidentalis* (above) nest in colonies on the Peruvian coast where their guano, or bird droppings, is collected and used as fertilizer.

Pelicans are superb fishers. Their tactics vary according to species and where they are fishing. The Brown Pelicans drop out of the sky onto the fish, catching them in their enormous pouched bills, which serve as fishing nets. Other species, if fishing in open water, will sometimes gather together some distance from the shore and form themselves into a half-circle. Then, swimming with military precision, they beat the water with their wings to drive the fish shorewards until they are trapped in shallow water. The whole group of pelicans will then simultaneously dip their bills into the water to scoop up the fish, repeating the movement again and again in perfect synchronization.

Most species of pelican nest on the ground, on islands or in marshland — wherever the fishing is plentiful. Their nests are roughly put together and the newly hatched chicks are very tiny, only about 3 inches (75 mm) long and quite helpless. Both parents take on the job of feeding the young until the chicks are strong enough to learn to push their heads into the pouches of the adults to feed themselves.

The valuable guano of the Brown Pelican provides a sound economic reason for its continued protection and its population in most areas is fairly stable. Several of the other species of pelican, however, notably the White Pelican used to be quite widespread in Europe but its range has shrunk to a fraction of what it was a century ago, and the only widespread colonies now are on the Danube Delta. The reason for this decline is that White Pelicans are very vulnerable to disturbance — any human intruders may easily cause a whole colony to desert their nests — and they are also very susceptible to predators. Another factor, possibly the most important, is that the available habitat has declined enormously over the last century; undisturbed marshes and reedbeds and lakes with suitable supplies of fish have disappeared all too rapidly.

There are three groups of white swans. The Mute Swan *Cygnus olor* (see pages 2-3), which is only found in the Old World and has a bright orange bill, is the Royal Bird of England and other countries in northern Europe and was once served at medieval banquets. The smallest species (above) is known in Europe as Bewick's Swan *Cygnus columbianus* (after the English naturalist and illustrator), and in North America as the Whistling Swan (because of the sound made by the wings in flight). The largest of the swans is the species known in America as the Trumpeter Swan, and in Europe as the Whooper Swan. As its name suggests, this species is often vocal in flight.

In myths and legends swans are common; usually they symbolize grace and beauty and are, of course, white. Black swans were quite unknown in the northern hemisphere until fairly recently. In Greek legend, Leda was ravished by Zeus when he took the shape of a swan, although in most other legends the swan symbolizes purity and innocence. The swan-knights of the Middle Ages, such as Lohengrin, undoubtedly gave rise to the popularity of the swan as a heraldic figure; Henry V's pennant at the Battle of Agincourt carried a swan, as did many other princely families in Europe, and today it still continues as an inn sign. In many stories, for example 'The Eleven Princes' by Hans Andersen and the story immortalized by Tchaikovsky in the ballet 'Swan Lake', swans are

enchanted princes waiting to be released from a spell. Whooper swans are probably the species which drew Apollo's sun-chariot across the sky and the mournful calling of migrating swans as they depart for the Arctic in spring also gave rise to the legend that they only sing before they die — their swan-song.

Centuries before the Black Swan was discovered in Australia, black swans were mentioned in myths; since the white swan usually symbolized purity and goodness, it was natural to make the symbol of evil and the underworld a black swan. The real Black Swan *Cygnus atratus* (above) is even now generally considered unlucky in many parts of the world, and for that reason it is rarely kept in parks.

In the late nineteenth century, Black Swans were imported into New Zealand and soon multiplied to almost plague proportions. The numbers have now stabilized to a certain extent and the swans are culled each year to maintain a reasonable population. The largest concentrations occur on Lakes Ellesmere and Whangape, at the former it has been estimated that there are about 60,000 birds. The Black-necked Swan *Cygnus Melanocoryphus* (top left) of South America would seem at first to be a 'missing link' between the black and white swans. However they have evolved quite separately and, although it is quite widely distributed in the southern parts of South America, very little is known about the details of its life.

Ducks and geese are among the most familiar of all birds, mainly because they have long been domesticated. Nowadays they are also popular as ornamental birds and many parks and gardens have small collections of exotic species.

Perhaps the most popular and exotic of all the ducks is the Mandarin Duck *Aix galericulata* (bottom left). As its name implies, it is oriental in origin, but it is now found in many parts of the world and has often gone wild.

The Greylag Goose *Anser anser*, shown landing on a lake (top left), is the ancestor of one of the two types of domestic goose (the other is the Oriental Swan-goose). Geese were probably the first birds to be domesticated, although it is not known exactly when. The Ancient Egyptians kept them and Homer wrote about them. In an Ancient Egyptian tomb discovered at Medum, which was built before the Great Pyramid of Giza, is a frieze depicting Greylag Geese, together with White-fronted and Red-breasted Geese *Branta ruficollis* (top right). Today, Red-breasted Geese only occur in large concentrations in Romania on the Black Sea coast. They breed in Siberia.

The Emperor Goose *Anser canegieus* (previous pages) has rarely been seen in the wild by ornithologists because its breeding grounds are confined to a small area in the far west of Alaska and the far east of Siberia. The photograph shows a nest site on the flat open wastes of the Alaskan tundra, and it also nests on coastal marshes and islands. Although birdwatchers have rarely seen the Emperor Goose, it is well known to the local Eskimos. During August the geese moult their flight feathers and the Eskimos take the opportunity to round up large numbers of the grounded birds for food.

One of the remarkable features of most species of ducklings and goslings is that when they hatch they become 'imprinted' with their mother and follow her in a little troop. The family of young Pochard *Aytha ferina* (bottom right) will follow their mother, but had they been reared by another species they would follow that bird instead.

The Anhinga *Anhinga anhinga* (above) is also often known as the snake-bird or darter. Both these names are derived from its long, snake-like neck which it thrusts forward in order to spear its prey. This fishing technique is unusual among birds; most fish-eating waterfowl grasp the fish in the bill, but the Anhinga impales the fish, comes to the surface and then stuns or kills its prey by hitting it against a rock or branch before swallowing it whole, head first.

Anhingas are found in tropical and sub-tropical regions throughout the world, and fossils have been discovered which suggest that its ancestry can be traced back some 80 million years to the Eocene period.

In general appearance, the Anhinga resembles a long-necked Cormorant, and in fact it shares several characteristics with the Cormorant. It is relatively heavy, lacking the air sacs which give many birds their buoyancy; this enables it to dive and stay submerged under water, but makes taking off from the water rather difficult. Also, unlike many other sorts of waterbirds, Anhingas (and Cormorants) lack an oil gland with which to keep their plumage greased and watertight. After a few swims the plumage is liable to become waterlogged and the Anhinga must climb out of the water. The photograph shows it in

a characteristic pose with its wings outstretched in the sun to dry.

The jacanas are a small family of birds related to the waders, and are found in approximately the same regions as the Anhinga; they are also often found in the same habitat. They are popularly known as 'lily-trotters' or 'lotus birds' because of their ability to walk on floating plants. They do this by spreading their weight across several lily pads on their enormously elongated toes. Jacanas vary in size from the Lesser Jacana *Micnoparra capensis* (right) of southern and eastern Africa, which is less than 6½ inches (170 mm) long, to the Pheasant-tailed Jacana of India and the Far East, which is over 20 inches (500 mm) long, including its tail.

Jacanas are so well adapted to a life on floating vegetation that even the nest is built among the lilies. The eggs have a waxy coating on the surface to protect them if the nest is ever flooded. An unusual feature of the breeding of the Pheasant-tailed Jacana is that the female is polyandrous and has several mates; she lays anything up to ten clutches of eggs a year and the various males are left to incubate the eggs and bring up the young while the female goes off in search of another mate.

Grebes are superbly adapted for a life in and under water. The feet are set well to the back of the sleek, streamlined body, which is insulated from the water by a dense downy plumage covered with watertight feathers. Instead of webbed feet, grebes have lobes of skin extending round each toe which increase the surface area of the feet and help propel the bird through the water.

The courtship displays of grebes are elaborate and beautiful to watch. Great-crested Grebes *Podiceps cristatus* (bottom left) approach each other, fanning their beautiful head feathers and, after bobbing and bowing in a variety of 'dances', often present each other with bits of pondweed, a symbol of nest-building.

As you can see in the photographs, grebes build floating nests which they anchor among the reeds. The young are quite unlike the parents in appearance; they are little striped chicks which the mother carries on her back for the first few days after hatching. You can see the chicks in the photograph (top left) of a Red-necked Grebe *Podiceps grisegena*.

The Eastern Swamphen *Porphyrio melanotus* (below) is found in most of Australia, except the west. Related to the familiar coots and moorhens (gallinules) it occurs in similar habitats around the margins of lakes and rivers, usually fairly close to cover. Swamphens sometimes gather in large numbers, although they are more usually seen in pairs or small flocks. The relatively long toes enable them to pick their way across floating vegetation and, as they search for the insects, molluscs and plants on which they feed, they bob their tails continuously. The nest is a rather untidy heap of reeds and other vegetation built on a tussock or small island, usually at the edge of the water.

Waders

To many birdwatchers the voice of the Curlew *Numenius arquata* (left) is symbolic of wild places and marshes. The virtually indescribable, ethereal trill, from which the bird takes its name, is certainly one of the most haunting of all bird calls.

The Curlew is a wading bird only found in the Old World (though there are several other closely related species in both the Old and the New World). It is generally associated with estuaries and mudflats, where it probes with its long downward-curving bill for worms and grubs. During the breeding season Curlews move inland from the estuaries and coasts to moors, heaths and even tundra, although they still prefer wet, boggy areas. The chicks have short bills and, like all other waders, are active from hatching, as can be seen in the photograph.

As soon as the brood have all hatched (which is usually completed within a few hours of the first one hatching), the parents lead the chicks away from the nest. At the approach of any danger, the chicks will scatter and then 'freeze', relying on their camouflage for protection.

Looking in silhouette rather like a Curlew with a straight bill, the Black-tailed Godwit *Limosa limosa* (below) in breeding plumage is certainly a more handsome bird. In Holland, Black-tailed Godwits are a characteristic sight on the polders in springtime and they are often very tame. At one time they were much more widespread in Europe, and were also probably quite common in many parts of Britain. The drainage and reclamation of the marshlands in the eighteenth century spelt disaster for the godwits, and by the middle of the nineteenth century they were more or less extinct in England and had disappeared from much of the rest of their range in Europe. Their popularity as a game bird led to their further destruction, and it is really only recently that a more enlightened attitude has halted their continued decline. Under strict protection, their numbers have increased in some areas and a few pairs have even managed to recolonize England, appearing in the fens on the east coast.

Early in the nineteenth century, the famous naturalist-artist John James Audubon described the Marbled Godwit *Limosa fedoa* (top left) flying down the Atlantic coast of America in vast flocks. Since then it has been severely hunted and its numbers have decreased rapidly, although today there are again some signs of an increase.

The Marbled Godwit breeds in the interior of North America on prairies and meadows. In the winter it migrates to the coast, where it is found on marshes and mudflats.

Another species which has been hunted to extinction in many parts of its range is the Avocet *Recurvirostra avosetta* (bottom left). In England, however, the Avocet has returned as a regular breeding bird after an absence of a century, probably mainly due to the fact that just across the North Sea in Holland there are very large colonies of Avocet which have flourished under strict protection.

The bold black and white plumage of the Avocet makes it a very conspicuous bird at the nest site, and for protection against predators it relies on the inaccessibility of its nest, generally nesting on islets in shallow lagoons. The nest is often well separated from the nearest cover, so that an approaching predator can easily be seen. If there is any sign of danger the Avocet will often leave the nest and rely on the eggs being protected by their camouflaged patterning. Once the chicks have hatched, the parents lead them away from the nest and, like most other waders, the chicks rely on their camouflage and ability to 'freeze' to protect them from predators. The parents also try to help the young by performing a 'distraction display'. Many species of birds perform these displays, one of the commonest of which is the 'broken wing' display. The parent bird trails one wing on the ground, fluttering as if the wing was broken, all the time leading away the would-be predator.

The Black-winged Stilt *Himantopus himantopus* (right) is thought to be fairly closely related to the Avocet. Both species have a very wide distribution and like the Avocet, the Black-winged Stilt is also declining in many parts of its range. Its plumage is rather variable and the birds found in New Zealand have entirely black plumage.

Hole~nesting birds

The four woodpeckers shown here are all found in Europe. The woodpecker family, however, is a very big one, distributed throughout most parts of the world, except Australia and New Guinea.

No birds are better equipped for their life on the trunk of a tree than the hole-chiselling woodpeckers. They have thick, straight, sharply pointed beaks, they can cling to the bark by means of their powerful claws and their strong stiff tail feathers help to support them in a vertical position as they chip and dig.

Another distinctive feature of woodpeckers is their exceptionally long tongue, often four or five times longer than the bill, with which they probe for the insects and grubs that infest trees. In some species, the tongue is either barbed or covered with a sticky substance to which the insects adhere.

On the whole, woodpeckers are solitary birds, rarely seen in flocks. In the woods, they systematically work their own trees, beginning at the base of the truck and moving upwards, hammering and chipping as they go.

The loud drumming of some species, which echoes through the woods like a pneumatic drill in the spring-time, is their proclamation that the courting season has begun. To attract a mate, the woodpecker selects a piece of dead wood or any object which is resonant and taps it vigorously and very rapidly with its beak.

As soon as the woodpeckers pair off they set about excavating a hole for their nest. The choice of a site depends on the size and strength of the birds' beaks. Some of the more powerful birds choose trees of very hard wood. The smaller, weaker woodpeckers often take the easy way out and make their nests in soft, rotten wood. Once the hole is excavated, it is sometimes lined with a few wood chippings and on these the hen lays her white, almost spherical, eggs.

It was once assumed that most hole-nesting birds laid white eggs because there was no need for camouflaging colour in a hidden nest. Recently, however, ornithologists have shown that in the gloom of the nest hole it is a definite advantage to have white eggs as it makes them easier to see and prevents accidental breakages. So, rather than just 'losing' their colour because it was useless, natural selection operated in favour of birds which laid paler eggs.

On the ground, woodpeckers hop about in an awkward clumsy way, but once in the air they have a beautiful undulating flight which is quickly recognized by birdwatchers.

The handsome Great Spotted Woodpecker *Dendrocopus major* (left) is the most widespread in Europe and is quite often seen in wooded parks. The Grey-headed Woodpecker *Picus canus* (top right) is far less common, usually living in mountainous regions. The only other greenish woodpecker found in Europe is the Green Woodpecker *Picus viridis* (bottom right), slightly larger than the Grey-headed and with more red on the crown. Smallest of the European woodpeckers is the black and white Lesser Spotted Woodpecker *Dendrocopus minor* (middle right); altogether there are over thirty species of spotted woodpeckers, mostly found in the Old World.

Kingfishers are widely distributed in most regions of the world, and are particularly abundant in the tropics. Although we usually associate kingfishers with watery habitats, a great many species are found well away from water. The kingfishers of the ponds, lakes and rivers, including the familiar brilliant blue kingfisher of Europe, feed almost exclusively on fish, although the larger species will also take amphibians and other aquatic animals, as well as a few insects.

One kingfisher which does not live near water is the Sacred Kingfisher *Halycon sancta* (top left) which is widely distributed in Australia, New Guinea, New Zealand and surrounding islands.

The Malachite Kingfisher *Alcedo cristata* (bottom left) occurs widely in Africa south of the Sahara. It is only 5½ inches (140 mm) long, of which over a quarter is taken up by the bright red bill. In spite of its brilliant plumage, it is often difficult to observe as it perches motionless in wait for its prey.

The Lesser Pied Kingfisher *Ceryle rudis* (top right) is also found in southern Africa, as well as in Asia Minor, the Middle East, India and Indo-China. It sometimes fishes from a convenient perch, like the branch in the photograph, but it also frequently hovers above the water at a height of 25 feet (7.6 m) or more. Small prey is swallowed immediately but larger fish have to be taken to a perch or stone to be battered to death. This species will also hunt over land for grasshoppers, locusts and other small prey. The Brown-hooded Kingfisher *Halycon albiventris* (bottom right) is another African species.

All kingfishers build their nests by tunnelling anything up to 3-10 feet (0.9-3 m) into clay or sandbanks before excavating the round nesting chamber. Sometimes they will even take over old termite nests. The parents never clean the nest which smells horribly as it becomes filled with stale fish, decaying fishbones and excrement.

The brilliantly coloured bee-eaters live in Africa, Asia, Australia and Europe and are often to be seen in flocks, flying among the tree-tops or perching on telegraph wires. The pictures show two typically beautiful bee-eaters, the Australian Rainbow Bee-eater *Merops ornatus* (above) and the African Red-throated Bee-eater *Merops bulocki* (top right).

Bee-eaters use their strong pointed beaks to excavate long tunnels in cliffs or sandbanks or sometimes into level ground, at the end of which they make their nests. They mostly nest in colonies.

As one would expect from their name, bee-eaters are especially fond of bees and wasps, which they catch on the wing. Their acrobatic flight as they dart and swoop is reminiscent of the swallow's, and in Australia they are sometimes also known by the delightful name of 'golden swallows'. Bees and wasps, however, do not always have top priority in their diet. One African species has a voracious appetite for locusts and another sometimes rides on the backs of bustards, rhinos and other plains

animals, swooping down to snap up the insects disturbed by the larger animals' feet.

The attractive Hoopoe *Upupa epops* (far right) takes its name from its distinctive call 'hoo-poo-poo'. It is a familiar sight in many parts of southern Europe, Africa and Asia and is an occasional but very welcome visitor to the British Isles. It has a magnificent crest which it can raise or lower.

The Hoopoe's reputation for bad house-keeping is even worse than that of the kingfisher. The parents make no attempt to keep the nest clean, and it is said that you can smell a Hoopoe's nest long before you come across it in its tree hollow.

In the Middle Ages the flesh of these birds was thought to cure all manner of ailments and they were regarded with superstitious awe by many country folk.

The Woodhoopoe *Phoeniculus purpureus* (right) is only found in Africa where it flies among the trees in small noisy groups. It has no actual song but instead makes a kind of grunting noise.

There are few birds of the tropical forests which are so quickly identified as the hornbills and toucans.

Some of the hornbills of the Old World are huge birds. The Great Hornbill *Buceros bicornis* (top left), one of the largest of the forest-dwellers, has a tail more than half its own length, anything up to 3 feet (0.9 m) long. The casque, or helmet, along its enormous bill is typical of some of the larger birds. The Yellow-billed Hornbill *Tockus flavirostris* (bottom left) is one of the smaller kinds of hornbill, with no casque on its bill.

Many of the species have a unique and fascinating way of protecting their nests from monkeys and tree snakes which would otherwise steal the eggs and attack the nestlings. When the hen has settled in her tree hollow, perhaps 100 feet (30 m) from the ground, the male bird starts sealing her in with a muddy paste-like mixture which soon becomes as hard as concrete. Often he is assisted by the hen from the inside. In order to feed his mate during her long confinement, the male leaves a narrow slit in the nest wall through which she can thrust her beak at mealtimes. Not only does the male faithfully attend to the female, after the chicks are hatched he takes care of their needs also. In some species, the hen may be imprisoned for as long as three months or until her family is half grown. More usually, with the male bird's help, she pecks her way out after a few weeks and joins her partner in taking care of the chicks. It has also been discovered recently that in some species the chicks help replaster the nest entrance after the hen has left.

The hole-nesting toucans of the American tropical forests vie with the hornbills in the size of their colourful bills, sometimes as long as their bodies. Like the hornbills, these bills, however, are not as heavy as they look, for the horny outer covering conceals a network of bony fibres which is very light. There does not seem to be any satisfactory explanation why the fruit-eating toucans should have evolved such gigantic bills.

Most toucans are smaller birds than hornbills. The gaudy Sulphur-breasted Toucan *Ramphastos sulfuratus* (top right) and the Toco Toucan *Ramphastos toco* (bottom right), two of the largest toucans, are roughly the same size as a crow.

Spectacular birds

The floor of the jungle forest is a dimly lit, twilight world, covered with dense undergrowth, and it is here that the showy pittas spend most of their time.

All 23 species are small, stumpy birds, about the size of a quail, with rounded wings and very short, stiff tails. Their plumage is a patchwork of bright colours, earning them the title of the most brilliant birds of the Old World. But the gaudy pittas lead hidden, secret lives as they skulk about under cover and their startling plumage is rarely seen at its best. They are solitary birds, nearly always seen on their own and so wary that the slightest noise will send them scurrying away into hiding. Only when darkness falls do they leave the forest floor and fly up into the trees to roost, and their shrill whistles can be heard as they call to each other from their perches.

The Noisy Pitta *Pitta versicolor* (below) is found in eastern Australia and southern New Guinea. In Australia pittas are sometimes known as 'jewel-thrushes', although they are in no way related to thrushes. The Noisy Pitta is also appropriately nicknamed the 'dragoon bird' because of its showy plumage.

The Blue-tailed, or Banded, Pitta *Pitta gaujana* (left) is a little-known species from Malaysia. Like so many of the pittas, its habits have not been studied, but it probably builds the same type of nest as the other species, a large ball-like structure made of bamboo leaves and other vegetation, rather untidily put together and lined with finer vegetation, such as root fibres.

Pittas are chiefly insect-eating, although the Noisy Pitta has a particular liking for snails. This bird has its own anvil, usually a stone, on which it cracks open the snails' shells.

Some pittas migrate and those that live in the more temperate regions of China, Japan and Australia fly to the tropics for the winter months.

The Eastern Bluebird *Sialia sialis* (top left) is widespread in eastern North America. In the more northerly parts of its range, its arrival heralds approaching spring, although in other areas it is more or less sedentary. The warbling song, as well as its attractive plumage, have made this species very popular and it is also approved of by farmers because it often nests in and around orchards, feeding largely on insects and other potential pests.

In Africa, there are a number of brilliantly coloured and iridescent species of starlings. The Lesser Blue-eared Starling *Lamprocolius chloropterus* (bottom right) belongs to a group of widespread and often common starlings. It is usually found in wooded areas of eastern and southern Africa.

The Satin Bowerbird *Ptilonorhynchus violaceus* (top right) is confined to Australia, New Guinea and a few nearby islands. During the breeding season, the male, which is about the size of a thrush, builds a bower in order to attract a mate. There are many different types of bower, but the Satin Bowerbird builds one of the 'avenue' type. It consists of a fairly solid mass of twigs which are laid out in two rows to form the avenue, rising to about 1 foot (30 cm) high and often nearly meeting overhead. The male is not content with this structure, however, and once it is complete he sets about decorating it. Blue is the Satin Bowerbird's favourite colour, but violets and purples are also acceptable, as well as green and yellow, and the male assiduously sets about collecting virtually any object he can find in these colours. In the 'natural' state he will mainly gather feathers which have been moulted by other birds, flowers, fruits and berries, but, since the Satin Bowerbird often lives near to people, he has taken to using a wide variety of waste material, such as coloured glass, paper, bottle tops and plastic. The total collection may contain a hundred or more objects. Strewing coloured objects around the bower is not the only way in which the Satin Bowerbird decorates, however; he is also one of the few birds in the world to actually employ a tool. Using a wad of bark, he 'paints' the bower with a mixture of charcoal and saliva, a rather inefficient mixture as it crumbles when it dries and has to be replaced more or less daily.

After the Satin Bowerbird has finished this elaborate construction a considerable amount of his time is spent merely in maintaining it, including keeping the avenue completely bare of any fallen leaves and chasing off any intruding males. He will also go on raiding trips to other bowers to try and steal more blue objects.

The tiny, brilliantly coloured blue wrens comprise eleven closely related species, all found in Australia or New Guinea. The species illustrated (bottom left) is the Splendid Wren *Malurus splendens*. Apart from their spectacular appearance, one of the most striking features of these birds is their social behaviour. They mostly live in small groups, consisting of one pair and a few camp-followers. During the breeding season the group will occupy a territory and together defend it against intruders. Although only the dominant pair actually produce eggs, all the others help to build the nest, incubate the eggs and feed the young.

In the tropics there have evolved a number of unrelated birds which feed primarily on the nectar of the myriad variety of blossoms. The most spectacular of the nectar-feeding birds are the hummingbirds. They are confined to the New World and, although a few species extend their range by migrating into temperate regions, they are essentially birds of the tropics.

The Broad-billed Hummingbirds *Cynanthus latirostris* (bottom right) and the Magnificent Hummingbird *Eugenes fulgens* (top right) are both shown here hovering, illustrating their remarkable powers of flight. When they are hovering, their wings may beat at 30 times a second or more, producing the humming sound. Many species can also actually fly backwards; they do this when backing away from a flower after hovering to extract the nectar.

The Broad-billed Hummingbird is a bare 3¼ inches (83 mm) long and is only found in a small area of Central America, mainly in Mexico, but also in the southern States of America. The Magnificent Hummingbird is one of the larger species, with a body of about 4 inches (100 mm) and a bill 1-1½ inches (25-38 mm) long. This species is also found in Central America.

In the Old World, the sunbirds are the equivalent of the hummingbirds. However, they are never quite as small as the smallest of the hummers, and their powers of flight are never quite as spectacular. Most species of sunbird occur in Africa, with a few in Asia. The species illustrated is the Orange-breasted Sunbird *Anthobaphes violacea* (left) of southern Africa.

In Australia and the Pacific there occurs another group of nectar-feeding birds, the honeyeaters. Honeyeaters are rather variable in appearance and habits. The Yellow-winged (or New Holland) Honeyeater *Meliornis novaehollandiae* (below) is a familiar bird in parts of southern and eastern Australia and Tasmania, where it is often to be seen in gardens feeding on the flowers of the spectacular Banksia or the flowers of the Eucalyptus tree. Like many other flower-feeding birds in Australia, honeyeaters tend to be nomadic, moving on when the supply of flowers in one place has been exhausted.

Parrots

The parrots are among the most popular birds in the world. Not only are they usually attractively plumaged, they also rank high in the avian intelligence stakes. This, and the ability of some species to mimic human speech, has made them popular as pets all over the world.

Parrots are essentially tropical birds, although a few species occur in temperate regions. The greatest variety is found in Australia, where parrots have evolved to fill a remarkable range of habitats. There are parrots that feed on nuts, fruit, blossoms, insects and even meat, and there are also nocturnal parrots.

The six species of rosella parakeets are among the most colourful of all Australia's many parrots. They are probably still actively evolving as several of the species show considerable variation in colour and pattern. The Eastern Rosella *Platycercus eximius* (left) was originally discovered near Rosehill in New South Wales and gave its name to the whole group of parakeets. Like all the Australian parrots, it is a hole-nesting species; it usually uses a hole in a tree or fence post or, more rarely, a rabbit burrow. Although it occasionally does some damage to fruit trees, it feeds mostly on grass seeds and berries.

The cockatoos are the largest of Australia's parrots, the Sulphur-crested Cockatoo *Cacatua sulphurea* (top right) growing to about 20 inches (500 mm) long. Although they are familiar as cage birds in many parts of the world, a single captive is a poor substitute for the magnificent spectacle of a flock of these birds flying free. Outside the breeding season, cockatoos often gather in flocks numbering several hundreds and can become pests if they start attacking crops. Normally, however, they are helpful to farmers as they eat weed seeds.

The fig parrots, no bigger than a sparrow, are among the smallest members of the parrot family. They are little-known birds of the tropical forests of New Guinea, Australia and nearby islands. As their name suggests, and the photograph shows, they are fruit-feeders, showing a preference for figs. The species illustrated (bottom right) is the Double-eyed Fig Parrot *Opopitta leadbeateri*, which takes its name from the broken ring of blue feathers around the eye.

Rainbow Lorikeets *Trichoglossus haematodus* (opposite page, bottom) are one of the commonest species of parrot within their range, which includes Australia, New Guinea and many surrounding islands. They often occur in vast flocks, wandering the countryside in search of food. Their principal food is nectar, which they extract by dabbing the blossoms of gum trees with their specially modified tongues. As the supply of blossom runs out in one area, they move on in search of a fresh supply. They also eat fruit and insects, and in some places have taken to raiding orchards. In Australia trays of sugared water are put out in parks to attract Rainbow Lorikeets and they have

become a regular and spectacular tourist attraction, as they soon become quite fearless and tame.

The lovebirds are a group of small dumpy parrots, eight of which are found in Africa and one in Madagascar. The Masked Lovebird *Agapornis personata* (sometimes known as the Yellow-collared Lovebird) (below) is well known as a cage bird, but in the wild has only a restricted distribution in East Africa. Despite its limited range, however, it is often very numerous, like most of the other lovebirds, and can become a pest, particularly on the millet crops. In the past, vast numbers were trapped to be sold abroad as pets. It has been calculated that in the 1880s less

than 3 per cent arrived in Europe, so bad were the transport conditions. Because of this a group of bird protectionists released some consignments of Masked Lovebirds at the port of Dar-es-Salaam in 1928, and the birds have since become established in the area.

The Plum, or Blossom-headed, Parakeet *Psittacula cyanocephala* (opposite page, top right) is found throughout India, Ceylon and eastwards to southern and eastern China. It is a very adaptable species, and is often found in cultivated areas.

Apart from Australia, the greatest variety of parrots is found in South America. They are found all over the continent, even the bleak Tierra del Fuego. The macaws are the largest of the New World parrots, and with their long graduated tails are an extremely impressive sight flying in flocks above the forest canopy. The Red and Green Macaw *Ara chloroptera* (above) is widely distributed, ranging from Panama southwards to Paraguay and northern Argentina. The other South American species of parrot illustrated is the Red-fan Parrot *Deroptyus accipitrinus* (opposite page, top left), a close relative of the more familiar and widespread Amazon Parrot. The Red-fan is found mainly in the tropical forests of the Amazon basin.

Birds of prey

The Secretary Bird *Sagittarius serpentarius* (left) is so different from all the other birds of prey that it is placed in a separate family of its own. Its long legs make it look more like a stork than a bird of prey, and in fact its methods of feeding and taking prey are very similar to those of storks and cranes. It strides across the grassy plains of Africa searching for snakes, lizards, locusts and other insects. The nest is usually built in a large, but fairly low, tree, often a flat-topped acacia. As you can see in the photograph, it is a massive platform of twigs about 6 feet (1.8 m) in diameter and 1 foot (30 cm) thick.

The King Vulture *Sarcorhamphus papa* (below right) is found in Central and South America and, like the other vultures of that continent, it is unrelated to the Old World vultures but closely related to the magnificent condors. Although the King Vulture is widespread, and in some areas quite common, very little is known about the bird's life history. It is thought that, like the Turkey Vulture of North America, its sense of smell may play an important part in helping it to locate the carrion on which it feeds, but the function of the colourful carbuncles around the bill is unknown.

Unlike many other buzzards, the Augur Buzzard *Buteo rufofuscus* (above right and overleaf) normally uses a vantage point to watch for its prey, rather than soaring in flight high above the ground. It will wait motionless for hours on a telegraph pole, dead tree or prominent rock before suddenly swooping down on an unsuspecting lizard or small mammal, or perhaps even an insect. Sometimes it will also hunt by slowly quartering a hillside, pausing occasionally to hover over a particular spot. During plagues of rodents and after fires, Augur Buzzards have been seen so bloated with food that they could hardly fly. In South Africa the Augur Buzzard is sometimes known as the Jackal Buzzard on account of its yelping, jackal-like call.

The Barn Owl *Tyto alba* (top left) almost certainly accounts for a large number of apparently ghostly apparitions recorded in churchyards. Flying on silent wings, ghostly white, and occasionally letting out a blood-curdling screech, it is easy to imagine that it is a lost soul as it disappears among the tombs.

Like most owls, but by no means all, the Barn Owl is normally nocturnal. However, it will also hunt by day, particularly when feeding young. Its prey in the northern hemisphere consists largely of rodents, and the photograph shows the parent owl taking a brown rat to its young in their belfry nest-site.

The Little Owl *Athene noctua* (bottom left) is largely insectivorous, as can be seen from the photograph, although it will also take considerably larger prey. Little Owls are only 8½ inches (220 mm) long, the same length as a starling, although the Little Owl is a dumpier bird. They nest mainly in tree holes, often in disused woodpeckers' nests, and also in rock clefts and gaps in the masonry of old buildings. It was the Little Owl which became the familiar of Pallas Athene and one of Athene's attributes was wisdom, an attribute which owls, with their binocular vision and generally rather 'human' expression, have acquired for no other good reason.

The Spotted Eagle Owl *Bubo africanus* (bottom right) is probably the most widespread of the Eagle Owl Group to be found in Africa south of the Sahara. It is also the smallest of the group, only growing to 11-15 inches (300-400 mm) long. Spotted Eagle Owls do not take very large prey, but are usually content with small rodents, lizards, etc.

The Wood Owl *Ciccaba woodfordii* illustrated (top right) is the only representative in Africa of a group otherwise confined to tropical America. As its name implies, it is found in forests. The illustration shows two well-grown chicks; normally, however, only one egg is laid.

The larger birds of prey do not all feed on large animals; surprisingly, some hunt fairly small species. The African Hawk Eagle *Hieraëtus spilogaster,* shown here shading its young from the midday sun (left), belongs to a group of birds which all take relatively small prey, and the African Hawk Eagle has acquired a reputation as a poultry thief. Verreaux's Eagle *Aquila verreauxi* (above), one of the most impressive of Africa's eagles with its predominantly jet-black plumage, feeds mainly on hyraxes. The hyrax is an animal thought to be distantly related to the elephants, but no bigger than a hare — it is, in fact, the cony of biblical times. Although Verreaux's Eagle has occasionally been accused of taking sheep, this seems unlikely as it only rarely takes even small antelope. However, on sheep farms where jackals have often been exterminated, hyraxes have usually become very abundant and, like most other eagles, this species will feed on sheep carrion. The photograph shows an adult Verreaux's Eagle feeding its recently hatched downy chick.

Several species of eagle have adapted to a diet almost exclusively of fish. The species illustrated, the White-breasted Fish Eagle *Haliaeetus leucogaster* (right), occurs from India and Ceylon right round through south-east Asia to Australia. Apart from fish, these eagles have also been known to take sea snakes and even small crocodiles, but their main diet is probably carrion, which they find floating down rivers or washed up on beaches.

Pigeons, grouse and doves

The game birds — the pheasants, partridges, grouse, quails and their relatives — are nearly all essentially ground-dwelling species, although many of them take to the trees to roost at night, and some species live in densely wooded areas.

The quail are the smallest birds in this group, and the Painted Quail *Excalfactoria chimensis* (top right) is about the same size as a sparrow. As can be imagined, the chicks, which usually number about four to seven, are minute on hatching. Yet, like all their relatives, the chicks of the Painted Quail are active within a few minutes of hatching, and are soon running around like some kind of microscopic poultry or feathery beetle. The Painted Quail is popular as an aviary bird, when it is usually referred to as the Chinese Painted Quail; a rather misleading name as it in fact occurs widely in the Far East, from western India across China and south through Malaysia to Australia, where it is found only along the western coast. The female lacks the distinctive coloration of the male and has the dull brown marking typical of most female game birds.

In contrast, the Californian Quail *Lophortyx californica* (left) is relatively large, growing to 8 inches (200 mm) long, nearly twice the size of the Painted Quail. Only the male has the head plumes. The Californian Quail is common in woodlands in the western United States, and is now also found in parks and cities.

The sandgrouse (bottom right) are more closely related to the pigeons than to the grouse and other gamebirds. Like the gamebirds, however, and unlike pigeons, the young are well developed on hatching and have well-camouflaged, downy plumage. Perhaps one of the most interesting features of the biology of the sand-grouse is their adaptation to life in very dry surroundings. In some of the desert-living species, the parent birds fly each day to the nearest water supply, where vast numbers of sand-grouse gather. The males soak their belly feathers in the water and take back water to the chicks, which then 'milk' the liquid from the sodden feathers. In one species of sandgrouse it has been found that the saturated feathers can carry fifteen to twenty times the bird's weight in water.

Best known of the three birds shown here is, of course, the Peacock *Pavo cristatus* (left) which typifies everything that is gorgeous and extravagant. The male bird's shimmering tail, decorated with the famous 'eye-spots', is really a train, his real tail acting as a support. The true home of the harsh-voiced Peacock is the forests of India and Ceylon, but peafowl have been bred in captivity for over 2000 years. In Greek mythology we frequently find mention of the Peacock and we are told in the Bible that King Solomon imported these exotic birds together with gold, silver, ivory and apes. Easily tamed, peafowl spend their days on the ground, flying into the trees at night to roost. The Peacock's glorious train is seen at its best when he spreads it out in courtship. Through the centuries, jewellers and painters have taken their inspiration from the proud Peacock.

The Satyr Tragopan *Tragopan satyra* (below) belongs to a highly specialized group of pheasants and is only found in the Himalayas. Apart from their glowing, beautifully patterned plumage, tragopans are interesting because, unlike other kinds of pheasant, they nest up in the trees instead of on the ground.

The breathtaking beauty of the stately Lady Amherst Pheasant *Chrysolophus amherstiae* (right), found in the Himalayas, has made it a very popular aviary bird. The hen, in sharp contrast to the cock, is nearly always rather drab in colour.

Members of the grouse family, which is found in the more northerly parts of the northern hemisphere, perform elaborate and spectacular displays during the breeding season. These displays, often involving several males, are known as 'leks' and are usually performed on special 'lekking grounds' or 'strutting grounds'. One of the most impressive of all the displays is performed by the Sage Grouse *Centrocercus urophasianus* (top right). Anything up to a hundred of the birds will gather at the lek, which is usually clear of any tall vegetation. Each male occupies his own territory and attempts to attract the females by his display. He begins by fanning his spiky tail vertically, then inflates the yellow air sacs on his breast, throws his head back into the neck feathers and arches the wings forward. In this contorted position, clearly shown in the photograph, the male 'dances' at the female, accompanying himself with noises produced by rubbing his feathers together, and by a bubbling note as air is released from the yellow air sacs.

The Sage Grouse was first described to science in 1827 by Prince Bonaparte, although it had been discovered over 20 years before. Prince Bonaparte, who was directly related to Napoleon but was far more interested in ornithology than politics, was one of the founding fathers of American ornithology.

The Greater Prairie Chicken *Tympanuchus cupido* also gathers in groups to perform its equally strange display (bottom right). The display starts with a short run, and the male then performs a rapid stamping 'dance' producing a drumming sound. He then raises his tail and spreads it, at the same time inflating the brightly coloured air sacs at the side of the head. While the sacs are being inflated, the bird produces a strange, resonant booming sound. The sacs are then let down, and the bird cackles like a farmyard chicken, leaping in the air. On landing, it chases after any males who may be nearby and they may indulge in short fights, striking each other with their wings.

The Greater Prairie Chicken was once much more numerous than it is at present. Until the mid-1920s it was quite abundant over much of its range east of the Rocky Mountains, but it is now reduced to isolated and heavily depleted local populations. Several factors have contributed to this decline, among them the spread of agriculture across the prairies, prairie fires during the breeding season and overshooting. The populations are now so rare that the International Union for the Conservation of Nature (IUCN) has listed them as rare and in need of conservation.

The Namaqua (or Masked) Dove *Oena capensis* (above) is a fairly small species, its long tail taking up a considerable proportion of its 11-inch (280 mm) length. It is widely distributed in Africa, mainly south of the Sahara, and inhabits fairly open country. It is often to be seen on the roadside, where it is very active, running about looking for food.

Although perhaps not quite as spectacular as the parrots, the diversity of the pigeons in south-east Asia and Australia is remarkable. The three species illustrated are all from this area and give some indication of the variety of pigeons that one is likely to see. The crowned pigeons are the largest of the family, and the diminutive Diamond Dove *Geopelia euneata*, not much bigger than a sparrow, is among the smallest of the world's pigeons.

The Diamond Dove (top left) takes its name from the small white spots which decorate its wings, but the bright salmon-red bare skin around the eyes is also a striking feature of the species. It is found in fairly arid areas in the centre of Australia, where it tries to nest fairly close to a water supply. The illustration shows a parent bird feeding the young at their nest in a Eucalyptus tree. Like many other pigeons, Diamond Doves produce a secretion in the crop, known as 'pigeon's milk', with which they feed the young for the first few days after hatching.

In contrast to the Diamond Dove, the three crowned pigeons, or gouras, may grow to 2½ feet long (800 mm), the size of a large chicken. Their impressive appearance is enhanced by a large but delicate lacy crest. Crowned pigeons are only found in the forests of New Guinea and a few adjacent islands. The three species are distinguished from each other mainly by the amount of maroon on the underparts and the colouring of the crest. The Victoria Crowned Pigeon *Goura victoria* (right) has a dark crest which is tipped with white. Although these beautiful and impressive birds are protected throughout most of their natural range, large numbers are still exported illegally; this is in spite of the fact that they can, and have, been bred in captivity.

The Crested Pigeon *Ocyphaps lophotes* (bottom left) has a similar distribution to the Diamond Dove, generally in rather arid country but always within reach of water. It usually visits the water shortly after sunrise and often returns in the evening to drink. Artificial lakes and cattle troughs have allowed Crested Pigeons to colonize new areas.

Seabirds

The Kittiwake *Rissa tridactyla* (left) is one of the characteristic seabirds of the north Atlantic, where it nests on precipitous cliffs, building a fairly bulky nest quite unlike that of any other species of gull. The base of the nest is constructed on a very narrow ledge from wet seaweed which, when dry, sticks firmly to the ledge. The sides of the nest are then built up out of grass, seaweed and mud until it is quite large, possibly even wider than the actual ledge; finally a grassy cup is built, into which the eggs are laid.

The gannets and boobies form a fairly closely knit group of seabirds which are found in most of the world's oceans. The gannets are found mainly in temperate and arctic waters, the boobies in tropical waters.

The gannet *Sula bassanus* (overleaf) is one of the relatively few birds which seems to be increasing its number and has probably more than doubled its population this century. This is almost certainly due to the decrease in human persecution; until the end of the last century, gannets were an important source of food.

A gannetry is very densely packed and in order to prevent fighting between neighbouring pairs and to keep the pairs together amid the apparent confusion of the colony, elaborate displays have developed. In the typical courtship display the male and female face each other with their wings opened, waving their heads and striking their bills against each other. Like many other birds, they also indulge in ritualized preening of each other. Before taking off, the birds stretch upwards, pointing their bills skyward, and utter a snoring sound (see photograph, middle right).

The Blue-footed Booby *Sula nebouxii* (top right) has a breeding range which extends from the west coast of tropical America to the Galapagos islands. In general appearance, its brown plumage makes it look rather like the immature birds of other boobies, but it can easily be distinguished by its brilliant blue feet. Although the Blue-footed Booby nests on the ground, as do the gannets, some of the other species nest in trees. Just as in the colder parts of the world the parent birds must brood the young to keep them warm, in tropical regions it is often necessary for the parents to shade the youngsters from the heat of the sun, as can be seen in the photograph.

Both the boobies and the albatrosses have been considered 'stupid' by sailors because they are so easy to attack and kill. Albatrosses have been given nicknames such as 'goney', 'gooney' and 'mollymawk'. They are only found in the Pacific and Antarctic Oceans, although in recent years they have been sighted with increasing regularity in the North Atlantic; perhaps one day in the near future they will colonize. The Black-browed Albatross *Diomeda melanophris* (bottom right) is one of the commonest of the species inhabiting the far south. It is a fairly large bird with an 8-foot (2.5 m) wingspan. It only comes to land in order to breed, spending the rest of its life far out at sea, gliding on the slightest breeze, unless completely becalmed. Towards the end of September, the Black-browed Albatrosses begin to return to their breeding colonies and start building their tower-like nests. A single egg is laid during October and is incubated for about two and a half months, and it is another three months or more before the youngster is ready to fly.

Gulls are among the most familiar and widespread of all seabirds. Of the fifty or so species, more than half breed in the northern hemisphere and several species have successfully adapted to man-made environments. One such species is the Herring Gull *Larus canus* (above). Outside the breeding season, Herring Gulls are often abundant well inland, where they are common scavengers on rubbish tips. They have also taken to nesting in buildings, even in heavily built-up areas such as the heart of central London.

In contrast, the Swallow-tailed Gull *Creagnus furcatus* (top right) has a tiny range, only occurring as a breeding bird on the Galapagos Islands in the Pacific and spending the winter on the Cocos Islands and the western coast of South America. The Swallow-tailed Gull is a handsomely marked species, standing out from most other gulls, which are rather similar to each other with little to distinguish them. Apart from its strikingly coloured plumage and deeply forked tail, its most distinctive feature are its eyes, which are unusually large and surrounded with a ring of red. The eyes can be moved forwards to give the bird binocular vision, for the Swallow-tailed Gull is nocturnal, possibly to avoid the depredations of the Frigate Bird, and it feeds mainly at night. Unlike most gulls, Swallow-tails only lay one egg and when it hatches the down of the chick is a uniform grey, lacking the

disruptive patterning which helps to camouflage other gull chicks. The uniform grey down is an excellent camouflage, however, when seen in context against the grey volcanic rocks of the Galapagos.

There are a number of gulls with dark heads (or hoods), occurring mainly in the northern hemisphere. In the Old World the most widespread and abundant of these is the Black-headed Gull *Larus ridibundus* (right). The name is slightly misleading as the head is in reality dark brown. (It is the Mediterranean Gull which has a truly black head.) Although the Black-headed Gull frequently nests on coastal marshes, estuaries and similar habitats, it is as a colonist of inland areas that it has become well known. Like the Herring Gull and other gulls, it has learnt to scavenge and today several thousand spend the winter in large cities, although at the turn of the century they were quite unusual. Until recently there was a colony nesting on a sewage farm next to London's Heathrow airport.

Black-headed Gulls prefer nesting on islands, where they build a fairly flimsy nest from grasses and debris; if, however, the ground is subject to flooding, a considerably more substantial nest may be built, rising a foot (300 mm) or more above ground level. Normally three eggs are laid, and for the first few days after hatching the young remain in the nest and are brooded by the parents.

Grotesque and awkward though the inflated throat pouch of a displaying male Frigate Bird *Fregata sp.* (top left) may look, normally it is one of the most agile of all birds. It is like some kind of giant swift, with a wingspan of about 7 feet (2.1 m), and outside the breeding season it spends the whole day on the wing. Although they are seabirds, Frigate Birds never settle on the water; their plumage is not watertight and would soon become waterlogged. They take their name from their airborne piratical habits; they rarely fish for themselves but chase other seabirds, twisting and turning until they force them to regurgitate their last meal, which the Frigate Bird then pounces on before it reaches the water. They also raid nesting colonies, and Frigate Birds never leave their own

chicks unguarded; they are not averse to cannibalism.

If the Frigate Birds are like a giant marine swift, then the terns are surely the sea-swallows. One of the most widely distributed terns is the Little Tern *Sterna albifrons* (above) which nests in Europe, North America, Africa, Asia and south to Australia. It is one of the smallest species, measuring only some 10 inches (250 mm) long.

The Arctic Tern *Sterna paradisea* (bottom left) is the world record-holder for long-distance flying. It nests in the far north, and after the breeding season migrates to the Antarctic waters. Arctic Terns are long-lived birds; ringing has shown that in some cases they live 25 or more years, which means that some Arctic Terns must travel over a million miles during their lifetime.

Penguins are birds of the southern oceans, similar in appearance to the unrelated auk family — guillemots (murres), razorbills, puffins and auks — of the north. The name penguin was originally applied as 'pinguin' to the Great Auk, a large flightless bird which was exterminated in the early nineteenth century.

Like the Great Auk, penguins are flightless. The largest penguin is the Emperor Penguin *Aptenodytes forsteri* (top left), with a total length of 4 feet (1.2 m). This bird has a remarkable life; it never sets foot on dry land, and breeds on the ice shelves in the bitter Antarctic winter, when temperatures drop as low as -40°F (-40°C).

The Gentoo Penguin *Pygosceus papua* (right), shown here with its chicks on Sigwy Island, is another species which breeds in Antarctica, although mainly on the islands around the continent. It also breeds on the Arctic ocean islands, such as South Georgia, the Falklands, and Kerguelen, and occasionally even as far north as New Zealand or Tasmania.

Members of the auk family not only often look like the penguins, they are undoubtedly undergoing similar evolutionary changes. Although not actually flightless like the Great Auk, most of the other species rarely fly long distances, but instead are strong swimmers, escaping from predators by diving under water.

One of the most widespread and common of the auk species is the Guillemot or Common Murre *Uria aalgae* (centre left). It often nests in vast colonies, usually mixed with other species of sea birds. No nest is made and the single egg is laid onto the bare rock of a narrow cliff ledge. The egg is very pointed at one end so that if it rolls it does so in an arc, which helps to prevent it rolling off the ledge.

The Puffin *Fratercula arctica* (below left) breeds on both sides of the North Atlantic, but unlike most other auks it nests underground, often using old rabbit burrows, although Puffins are powerful diggers themselves. The gay, colourful bill with which Puffins are adorned during the breeding season has earned them the nickname 'sea-parrot'. The bill is not merely decorative, it is also useful when gathering fish for hungry youngsters; a dozen or more small fish can be lined up along its length.

Acknowledgments

The publishers would like to thank the following organizations and individuals for their kind permission to reproduce the pictures in this book: Ardea 4–5, 10, 27 above, 31 below, (D. Avon & T. Tilford) 16 above, 17 above, 21 below, 66, 68 above right, 78, 79 above, (I. R. Bearnes) 13 below, (H. & J. Beste), 67 below, 77 below, (B. Bevan) 53 centre, (P. Blesdale) 56–57 above, (R. J. C. Blewitt) 53 below, (R. M. Bloomfield) 57 below right, 77 above, (J. B. & S. Bottomley) 46 below, 54 below, (G. J. Brockhuysen) 50 below, (R. Bunge) 59 below, 69 above, (D. Burgess) 17 below, 18 above, 18 below, 19, (E. Burgess) 62 above, (G. Chapman) 61, 85, (F. Collett) 39, 47, (W. Curther) 53 above, (M. D. England) 31 above, 35 above, (K. Fink) 16 below, 42 below, 50 above, 58 above, 71 below, 81 above, 81 below, 83 above, (R. L. Fleming) 71 above, (W. Free) 87 above, (P. Germain) 12 below, 90, (C. Knights) 38 below, (P. Lamb) 49, (E. Linders) 84 below, (E. Mickleburgh) 87 below, 94 above, 95, (P. Morris) 37, 60, (C. Mylne) 82, 87 centre, (R. Richter) 91 below, (S. Roberts) 9 above, (P. Steyn) 1, 64 above, 70, 75 above, 88–89, (W. R. Taylor) 54 above, (A. Warren) 91 above, (A. Weaving) 11 above, 33, 45, 63 below, 72–73, (W. Weisser) 65 above, 65 below, (J. Wight) 55 above, (J. S. Wightman) 68 below, 79 below, (T. Willcock) 83 below.
Bruce Coleman (J. & D. Bartlett) 68 above left.
NHPA (A. Anderson) 86, (D. Baglin) 25, (I. Bennett) 23, (F. Blackburn) 9 below, 14 below, 48, (J. Blossom) 67 above, 80, (S. Dalton) 20 below, 21 above, 34, 35 below, 44, 74 above, 74 below, 94 below, 94 centre, (E. Elms) 69 below, (F. Greenaway) 93, (J. Good) 42 above, 43 below, 52, (B. Hawkes) 2–3, 28, 41 above, 46 below, 92 below, (E. A. Janes) 13 above, 15, (P. Johnson) 12 above, 24, 29, 32 below, 55 below, 56–57 below, 75 below, 76, (M. Morecombe) 6–7, 8, 14 above, 32 above, 62 below, 64 below, (K. B. Newman) 11 below, 22, 27 below, 32 above, 58 below, G. Pizzey) 26, (P. Scott) 20 above, 38 above, 43 above, 83, 92 above, (A.G. Wells) 51, 56 left, 84 below.
Picturepoint 96.
B. Risdon 36, 59 above.
Front jacket: B. Risdon
Back jacket: Ardea (P. Steyn).
Endpapers: Bruce Coleman (A. J. Deane).

Index